Earth Matters

Environmental Vocabulary Games

and Other Activities

a Supplemental Resouce for

Our Living Planet

and

Going Green

Raymond C. Clark and Anne Siebert

PRO LINGUA ASSOCIATES

Contents

Pro Lingua Associates, Publishers

P.O. Box 1348, Brattleboro, Vermont 05302 USA

Office: 802-257-7779, Orders: 800-366- 4775

Email: info@ProLinguaAssociates.com • WebStore: www.ProLinguaAssociates.com

SAN: 216-0579

Copyright © 2009 by Raymond C. Clark and Anne Siebert

ISBN 13: 978-0-86647-296-8; 10: 0-86647-296-7

Printed in the United States of America • First edition, first printing 2009.

Introduction for the Teacher

This Teacher's Supplement contains games and activities for the two-book series, **Earth Matters**. The two books are intended to be used in sequence, although they may be used independently of each other. The recommended sequence is to use *Our Living Planet* first and *Going Green* second. *Our Living Planet* is a basic introduction to the physical geography, plant and animal life, and human presence on Earth. The basic concepts and vocabulary in *Our Living Planet* set the stage for *Going Green*, where environmental problems are described and solutions are suggested.

The contents of this booklet are photocopyable for classroom use. Several of the games may be used over and over again, and so laminating the material, although time-consuming, will make the effort worthwhile in the long run.

The descriptions and procedures for the games and activities, described below, are the same for both books. The contents, of course, differ. The material on pages 4 – 41 is intended for *Our Living Planet*. Pages 42 – 78 are for *Going Green*. Many of the games are set up as a page of 12 rectangles with phrases and words in the rectangle. We will refer to these rectangles as "cards," because they can be made into a kind of game card.

Phrase Match pages 4 and 42

Preparation:
There are two pages of words/phrases that are combined to form a sentence. The first part of the sentence is on the first page, and the end of the sentence is on the second page. Photocopy the first page. The cards on this page (with the first parts of the sentences) are numbered from 1 – 12. On the backside of the page, write the same numbers so that card 1 has "1" on its back, etc. Then photocopy the second page with the ends of the sentences. On the backside write the numbers 13-24 that appear on the front side. At this point, it is optional but advisable to laminate the uncut sheets. Then cut them into 24 rectangles. Lay the rectangles out on a table, separating the two parts of the sentence, as below:

1	2	3		13	14	15
4	5	6		16	17	18
7	8	9		19	20	21
10	11	12		22	23	24

Alternatively, after photocopying the two sheets, cut them up into 24 rectangles and paste them on index cards. Then write the numbers 1-24 on the backs of the cards.

Procedure:
Lay the 24 cards/pieces out on a table with the numbers showing, from 1 -24. Taking turns, students call out two numbers, trying to make a match. Have the students choose a number from 1-12 (the beginning of the sentence) and then choose a number from 13-24. If the two numbers do not make a match, the result will be a nonsense sentence. The cards are turned back over again, and the turn passes to the next student. When a match is made, the cards are removed from the layout and the turn passes to the next student.

Contents: The three phrase match games are played after units 3, 6, and 10.

Word Match ✿ pages 10 and 48

Similar to the phrase match, there are three word match games to be played after units 3, 6, and 10. The match asks the students to match two forms of the same word, for example, "sun-sunny." When a student makes a match, they should try to use both words in a sentence. For example, "I can see the sun. It's a sunny day." With these games, it is not necessary to separate the two matching words as in the diagram above. Simply copy the number on the face of the card onto the back of the card.

Bingo ✿ pages 16 and 54

Preparation:

Photocopy the bingo card with its word list. Each student gets a card. They then choose words from the list to fill out their cards by writing in additional words. They should not use the same word twice.

Procedure:

Using both the words given on the card and the words on the list, call out words one at a time. Keep track of the words you call out. When someone claims "bingo," have them read their words aloud. You can also ask them to use their words in a sentence. You may want to make more than one card for each student so that the game can be played more than once. A prize for the winner adds a bit of fun to the game.

Contents: There are five different bingo cards to be used after units 2,4,6,8, and 10.

Line-up ✿ pages 21 and 59

Preparation:

Photocopy the word cards, and as in the matching game, cut them into 12 rectangles, optionally laminating them before cutting.

Procedure:

Give each student a card. There are 12 cards. If you have more than 12 students, some will have to play as a pair. If you have fewer than 12 students, you may want to give some students two cards. Then have the students physically line up according to the instructions. In many cases there will be discussion and disagreement; that's part of the point of the game – to get people talking. However, they have to arrive at a final line-up. Compare their line-up with the answer. If some students have more than one card, instead of doing a physical line-up, they can lay their cards out on a table, chalk tray, or floor.

Contents:

The line-up pages may be used as independent activities. If you are coordinating this activity with one of the books, there is a note on each page indicating when to use the activity with the book. The answers are on pages 39 – 40 and 76 – 77.

Crosswords pages 26 and 63

Preparation:

Photocopy the crossword page and give it to the students.

Procedure:

You may choose to give the crosswords to pairs of students so that they practice conversation as they work together to find the solution.

Contents:

There are three different crosswords, to be used after units 3, 6, and 10. The solutions are available on pages 41 and 78.

Verb Cards pages 29 and 66

Preparation:

Photocopy the verb card pages and (optionally) laminate and/or paste them on index cards.

Procedure:

The cards may be used in a variety of ways. If you make multiple copies of the page, you can have two, three, four, or even five small groups, each working with a set and quizzing each other on the meaning and use of the verb. (**Suggestion:** If you do make multiple copies, it is a good idea to copy each set on a different color paper so they don't get mixed up.) You can also have a competition with teams. A team member takes a card from the pile and, with help from teammates, defines the word and uses it in a sentence.

Contents:

Each verb card has a number that indicates the unit in which the verb is introduced. You may sort the cards into sets. For example, after unit 3, your students can work with verbs from units 1 through 3. After unit 5, you could make a set of unit 4 and 5 verb cards, or you could use unit 1 through 5 verb cards, providing review. As a final review, you may use all the cards.

Quiz Cards pages 33 and 70

Preparation:

Photocopy the cards and optionally either laminate them or paste them on index cards or both. You may wish to make multiple sets allowing small groups each to have a set; it is useful to use different colored paper for each set to keep them from getting mixed up.

Procedure:

Each card has both the question and the answer. This allows the students to quiz each other. For example, put a pile of cards on the table. One student pulls a card and asks another the question. The student holding the card has the answer. Some students may quibble with the answer given. Allow them to discuss the matter; it is good practice. If need be, you serve as the judge. The cards can be used by competing teams with you keeping score on a blackboard scoreboard like a "pyramids" or "hangman" diagram.

Contents: There are two sets of 36 cards to be used after units 6 and 10.

Phrase Match Game for Units 1-3

Our sun is ___1	Venus ___7
Our moon is ___2	Mars ___8
Our galaxy ___3	A globe ___9
Our planet ___4	Earth ___10
Gravity ___5	A stone ___11
An orbit ___6	Earth's core is ___12

Earth Matters & Our Living Planet *(side margin)*

PHRASE MATCH GAME FOR UNITS 1-3

is a star. <div align="right">7</div>	is very hot. <div align="right">5</div>
a satellite. <div align="right">12</div>	is very cold. <div align="right">6</div>
is the Milky Way. <div align="right">9</div>	is a sphere. <div align="right">3</div>
is Earth. <div align="right">10</div>	is tilted. <div align="right">4</div>
is a force. <div align="right">1</div>	is a rock. <div align="right">8</div>
is a circular path. <div align="right">11</div>	a solid ball. <div align="right">2</div>

Phrase Match Game for Units 4-6

There are 1	Rain and snow are 7
Nitrogen is 2	Meteorologists can 8
There is 3	Earth's climate 9
Carbon gases are 4	Ocean water is 10
Liquids can 5	A strait is 11
Smog is 6	The poles 12

Earth Matters ❀ Our Living Planet

PHRASE MATCH GAME FOR UNITS 4-6

gases in the atmosphere. 11	precipitation. 1
a gas. 5	predict the weather. 6
oxygen in the air. 4	can change. 7
greenhouse gases. 3	very salty. 8
flow. 2	very narrow. 9
smoke and fog. 12	are melting. 10

Earth Matters ❀ Our Living Planet

Earth Matters ❀ Our Living Planet

A reservoir 1	Animal life 7
A dam forms 2	Female mammals 8
A river deposits 3	Many animals 9
Water vapor 4	We burn 10
A rainforest gets 5	Solar energy 11
People 6	Modern humans are 12

PHRASE MATCH GAME FOR UNITS 7-10

holds water.	has evolved.
9	3
a reservoir.	nurse their babies.
4	12
alluvial soil.	are endangered.
10	1
is a gas.	fossil fuels.
5	2
a lot of rain.	is renewable.
11	7
need fuel.	Homo sapiens.
8	6

WORD MATCH GAME FOR UNITS 1-3

circle 1	pole 10
sun 15	season 5
star 13	rotate 14
fun 17	sand 24
continent 3	dust 21
cloud 7	wind 11

Earth Matters 🌸 Our Living Planet

circular 22	polar 4
sunny 18	seasonal 20
starry 12	rotation 9
funny 2	sandy 23
continental 16	dusty 19
cloudy 8	windy 6

WORD MATCH GAME FOR UNITS 4-6

solid 10	climate 22
fog 5	damp 18
mix 8	glacier 9
moist 24	freeze 23
smog 21	salt 19
temperate 11	shine 6

Earth Matters & Our Living Planet

WORD MATCH GAME FOR UNITS 4-6

solidify	climatic
4	7
foggy	dampness
20	3
mixture	glacial
12	17
moisture	frozen
2	13
smoggy	salty
16	1
temperature	shiny
14	15

Earth Matters ❀ Our Living Planet

WORD MATCH GAME FOR UNITS 7-10

precipitate 7	estimate 16
erode 11	adopt 17
condense 14	solve 19
degrade 6	migrate 24
extinct 3	pollute 2
evolve 21	forest 23

Word Match Game for Units 7-10

precipitation 13	estimation 18
erosion 8	adoption 20
condensation 12	solution 1
degradation 9	migration 10
extinction 15	pollution 22
evolution 5	deforestation 4

Earth Matters ❀ Our Living Planet

BINGO GAME #1 FOR UNITS 1-2

				globe
			orbit	
		Earth		
	gravity			
to circle				

air	hemisphere	solar system
axis	ice	space
cloud	Milky Way	sphere
continent	ocean	star
equator	planet	sun
to float	pole	sunrise
funny	satellite	sunset
galaxy	season	

Bingo Game #2 for Units 3-4

				carbon
			core	
		nitrogen		
	oxygen			
gas				

atmosphere	mixture	solid
to crack	moisture	stone
crust	organic	substance
dust	pebble	temperature
to erupt	pressure	vegetation
greenhouse	sand	volcano
to grind	smog	warm
iron	soil	wind
liquid		

Bingo Game #3 for Units 5-6

				climate
			damp	
		to dissolve		
	to evaporate			
to flood				

continental	meteorology	sea level
current	moonlight	seacoast
fog	precipitation	shiny
glacier	to predict	strait
Gulf Stream	salinity	temperate
humidity	salty	tropical
melt	sea	zone

				agriculture
			alluvial	
		arid		
	basin			
biosphere				

border	delta	island
brook	to depend on	rainforest
to condense	to deposit	reservoir
to cut down	essential	to shrink
cycle	to flow	silt
deforestation	freshwater	stream
to degrade	fuel	vapor

Earth Matters ❀ Our Living Planet

BINGO GAME #5 FOR UNITS 9-10

				ancestor
			being	
		complex		
	to develop			
dinosaur				

to adopt	extinct	physically
endangered	fossil	primitive
energy	hydroelectric	renewable
to establish	mammal	reptile
to estimate	migration	solar
evidence	to nurse	solution
to evolve	organism	technology

LINE-UP #1
THE SOLAR SYSTEM – TO BE DONE AFTER UNIT 1

SUN	MARS
MERCURY	JUPITER
VENUS	SATURN
EARTH	URANUS
EARTH'S MOON	NEPTUNE
INTERNATIONAL SPACE STATION	PLUTO

Direction: Line up according to the distance from the sun from closest to farthest.

Notes: Earth's moon and the Intentional Space Station are tricky because they can be on either side of Earth. Although there is some debate, Pluto is no longer considered a planet.

Answers on page 39.

Mount Everest – Nepal/Tibet	Matterhorn – Switzerland
Aconcagua – Argentina	Mount Whitney – California
Denali – Alaska	Mount Rainier – Washington
Mount Logan – Canada	Ararat - Turkey
Pico de Orizaba – Mexico	Grand Teton – Wyoming
Mont Blanc – France/Italy	Olympus – Greece

Direction: Line up according to elevation

Answers on page 39.

LINE-UP #3
SEAS AND OCEANS – TO BE DONE AFTER UNIT 6

Pacific Ocean	Caribbean Sea
Atlantic Ocean	South China Sea
Indian Ocean	Bering Sea
Southern Ocean	Gulf of Mexico
Arctic Ocean	Red Sea
Mediterranean Sea	Baltic Sea

Direction: Line up according to the size of the seas and oceans.

Answers on page 40.

Earth Matters ❀ Our Living Planet

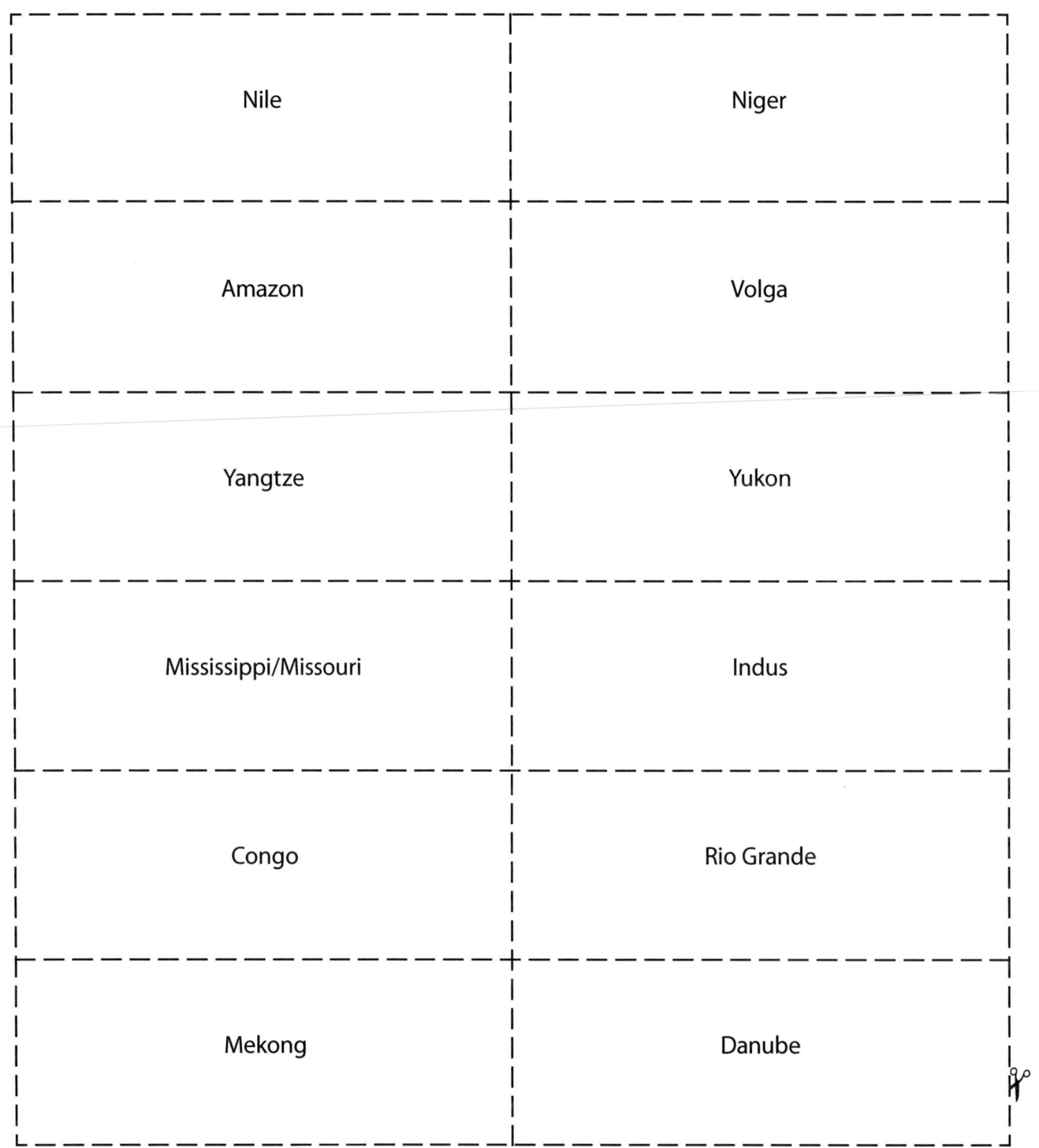

Nile	Niger
Amazon	Volga
Yangtze	Yukon
Mississippi/Missouri	Indus
Congo	Rio Grande
Mekong	Danube

Direction: Line up according to the length of the river.

Answers on page 40.

Tokyo	Lagos
Mexico City	Los Angeles
Mumbai	Calcutta
Sao Paulo	Buenos Aires
New York City	Seoul
Shanghai	Beijing

Direction: Line up according to the size of the population.

Answers on page 40.

CROSSWORD #1 – TO BE DONE AFTER UNIT 3

Across

2 Turning around
6 _____ ice caps
8 Half a globe
11 Connects the poles
13 _____, went, gone
15 Earth's surface
16 Earth's center

Down

1 The snow and ice at the poles
3 Natural; no chemicals
4 Not far
5 _____ up into pieces
7 We breathe it
9 Earth is one
10 A sphere
12 Earth is in it
14 It gives heat and light

CROSSWORD #2 – TO BE DONE AFTER UNIT 6

Across

3   A river in the ocean
5   _____ three o'clock (preposition)
8   Every
10 Our gaseous skin
14 Not liquid or a gas
15 We breathe it
16 Watery
17 It falls from the sky
19 Frozen water
20 Cloud at the ground
21 Seawater tastes _____

Down

1   A connector like "and"
2   Ice does this in the spring
3   A dioxide
4   A drink
6   Covering with water
7   A huge field of ice
9   A metal in Earth's core
11 To tell before it happens
12 A sound in "hiss"
13 The sound of one of these: J, K, L, M, N
18 Not far
20 Not near

CROSSWORD #3 – TO BE DONE AFTER UNIT 10

Earth Matters ❀ *Our Living Planet*

Across

1 Land surrounded by water
5 It contains things
7 To change with time
9 A polluter
10 Clouds at the ground
11 Not fast
12 Dear _____,
14 A color
16 One kind of energy
18 Quiet
19 See 5 down
20 The Caspian is one
21 Earth's living things
25 _____ Monday (preposition)
26 _____ two o'clock (preposition)
27 Not yesterday
28 We need it

Down

2 Mediterranean _____
3 Cutting all the trees
4 A friendly animal
5 An important verb
6 Not far
8 A letter and a sound
11 Become smaller
12 Bigger than a brook
13 A circle
15 A river's mouth
17 Opposite of "go"
19 The Amazon is one
22 A number
23 Horses eat it
24 Extra-Terrestrial

Verb Cards

circle 1	set 1
float 1	erupt 3
tilt 1	crack 3
rotate 1	break up 3
inhabit 1	grind 3
rise 1	dig 3

Verb Cards

breathe	retire
4	5
surround	dissolve
4	6
bathe	evaporate
4	6
change	melt
5	6
control	flood
5	6
predict	shine
5	6

Verb Cards

flow 7	shrink 7
condense 7	depend on 8
precipitate 7	degrade 8
deposit 7	cut down 8
scare 7	trim 8
drown 7	transplant 8

Verb Cards

develop 9	migrate 10
evolve 9	pollute 10
estimate 9	settle down 10
abandon 9	consume 10
adopt 9	toss 10
care for 9	burn 10

QUIZ CARDS – TO BE USED AFTER UNIT 6

1 How many planets are there?

eight

7 Why are Earth's poles white when seen from space?

They are covered with snow and ice.

2 Our galaxy is called _____

the Milky Way

8 What is Earth's axis?

a line through the center of Earth from pole to pole

3 What's the name of our path around the sun?

our orbit

9 What causes night and day?

The rotation of the earth

4 What force keeps us in our orbit?

gravity

10 What is another word for "sphere?"

ball, globe

5 Which planet is hotter, Venus or Mars?

Venus

11 What color is Earth from space?

brown, green, and white

6 What is the name of Earth's satellite?

the moon

12 How would you describe the equator?

It's like a belt around Earth's middle.

Earth Matters ❀ Our Living Planet

Earth Matters ❀ Our Living Planet

13 Is Earth's core solid or liquid?

It's solid.

19 What is Earth's atmosphere?

(a number of) gases

14 What is Earth's core made of ?

iron and nickel

20 What is air pressure?

the weight of air on the surface

15 Solid rock can be broken into pieces.
 What are they called?

stones, pebbles, sand, and dust

21 What are the two common gases in air?

nitrogen and oxygen

16 Which is larger, a stone or a pebble?

a stone

22 What is fog?

*moisture (water) in the air/
a cloud at the ground*

17 What does vegetation need in
 order to grow?

soil and water

23 What is smog?

fog and smoke

8 What is dust?

very small pieces of rock

24 What gas do we humans have to have?

oxygen

QUIZ CARDS – TO BE USED AFTER UNIT 6

25 What does a meteorologist do?

He predicts the weather.

31 What is NaCl?

common salt, sodium chloride

26 What is precipitation?

rain and snow

32 What is a strait?

a narrow body of water

27 What does relative humidity measure?

moisture or dampness in the air

33 Where is the Gulf Stream?

in the Atlantic Ocean

28 Where do we find tropical climates?

near the equator

34 What is an ocean current?

It's like a river in the ocean.

29 What are the names of the climatic zones between the equator and the poles?

temperate and continental

35 Does salt evaporate?

No, it doesn't.

30 When the relative humidity is high does it feel muggy or dry?

muggy

36 What happens when the poles melt?

Sea level rises and the coasts are flooded.

Earth Matters ❀ Our Living Planet

Quiz Cards – to be used after Unit 10

1 What is evaporated water called ?

(water) vapor

7 Is freshwater salty?

no

2 What does condensed water vapor form?

clouds

8 What causes erosion?

flowing water (brooks, streams, rivers)

3 Rain and snow are called _____.

precipitation

9 Where do we find deltas?

at river mouths

4 Which is bigger, a brook or a stream?

a stream

10 What does the biosphere include?

animal and plant life

5 What does a dam form?

a reservoir

11 Why do we need trees and bushes?

they create oxygen

6 Why are reservoirs shrinking?

cities are using more and more water

12 What does arid mean?

dry

13 Very dry places are called _____.

deserts

19 What is an amoeba?

a single-cell organism

14 Where is the biggest tropical rainforest?

Amazon River basin, Brazil

20 What kind of soil is deposited by rivers?

alluvial soil

15 What is deforestation?

cutting down trees

21 When did the first single-cell organisms develop?

about four billon years ago

16 What are islands?

land surrounded by water

22 Do any mammals lay eggs?

some do (most don't)

17 Why do Haitians cut down their forests?

for fuel

23 What is a fossil?

bones "frozen" in rocks

18 Is the Sahara Desert growing or shrinking?

growing

24 What can happen to endangered animals?

They can become extinct.

QUIZ CARDS – TO BE USED AFTER UNIT 10

25 When did primitive human beings live?

about two million years ago

31 Burning fossil fuels causes _____.

global warming

26 When did Homo sapiens evolve?

about 200,000 years ago

32 Humans need what to survive?

energy

27 Where did Homo sapiens develop?

Africa

33 What came first, early humans or dinosaurs?

dinosaurs

28 When did humans migrate to Asia?

about 100,000 years ago

34 Are dinosaurs mammals or reptiles?

reptiles

29 When did Asians migrate to the Americas?

about 18,500 years ago

35 What does Homo sapiens mean?

wise humans

30 Name three forms of renewable energy.

solar, hydroelectric, wind

36 On what continent do most human beings live?

Asia

ANSWERS FOR THE LINE-UPS

Answers for Line-up #1 on page 21

SUN
MERCURY
VENUS
EARTH
EARTH'S MOON
INTERNATIONAL SPACE STATION
MARS
JUPITER
SATURN
URANUS
NEPTUNE
PLUTO

Note: Earth's moon and the International Space Station are tricky because they can be on either side of Earth. Although there is some debate, Pluto is no longer considered a planet.

Answers for Line-up #2 on page 22

Note: These are not the highest in the world (except Everest). Most of the highest peaks are in the Himalayas. The elevations are below.

Mount Everest – Nepal/Tibet	29,035
Aconcagua – Argentina	22,841
Denali – Alaska	20,320
Mount Logan – Canada	19,551
Pico de Orizaba – Mexico	18,490
Mont Blanc – France/Italy	15,782
Matterhorn – Switzerlnd	14,690
Mount Whitney – California	14,505
Mount Rainier – Washington	14,411
Ararat – Turkey	13,780
Grand Teton – Wyoming	13,770
Olympus – Greece	9,570

ANSWERS FOR THE LINE-UPS

Answers for Line-up #3 on page 23

Note: The areas in square miles are below.
The Mediterranean includes the Black Sea.

Pacific Ocean	60,060,700
Atlantic Ocean	29,637,900
Indian Ocean	26,469,500
Southern Ocean	7,848,300
Arctic Ocean	5,427,000
Mediterranean Sea	1,144,800
Caribbean Sea	1,049,500
South China Sea	895,400
Bering Sea	884,900
Gulf of Mexico	615,000
Red Sea	169,100
Baltic Sea	163,000

Answers for Line-up #4 on page 24

Note: The length is in miles. These are not
the longest. They are well-known
rivers .

Nile	4,135
Amazon	3,980
Yangtze	3,917
Mississippi/Missouri	3,870
Congo	2,914
Mekong	2,600
Niger	2,590
Volga	2,266
Yukon	1,980
Indus	1,976
Rio Grande	1,900
Danube	1,771

Answers for Line-up #5 on page 25

Note: The numbers below are in millions.
Based on metropolitan area.
2008 estimate.

Tokyo	28,025
Mexico City	18,131
Mumbai	18,042
Sao Paulo	17,711
New York City	16,626
Shanghai	14,173
Lagos	13,488
Los Angeles	13,129
Calcutta	12,900
Buenos Aires	12,431
Seoul	12,215
Beijing	12,033

Source: www.worldatlas.com

Earth Matters ❀ Our Living Planet

Answers for the Crosswords

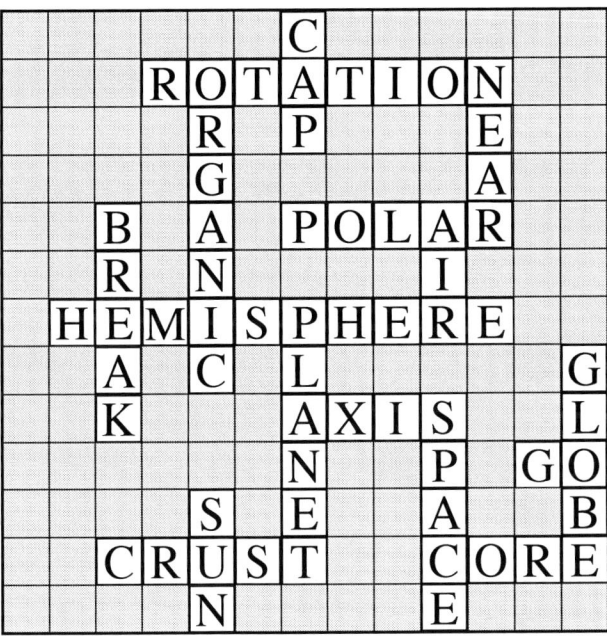

Crossword #1 – *to be done after Unit 3*
Puzzle on pages 26

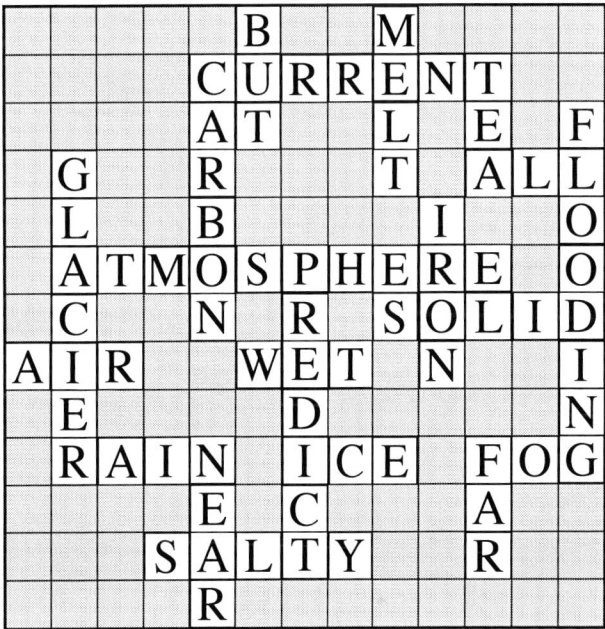

Crossword #2 – *to be done after Unit 6*
Puzzle on pages 27

Crossword #3 – *to be done after Unit 10*
Puzzle on pages 28

Phrase Match Game for Units 1-3

Our electric bill 1	An air filter 7
CFLs 2	Throw it 8
A computer 3	Water is 9
Please don't 4	A leaky faucet 10
Myths are 5	Let's take care of 11
One ton 6	Recycling means 12

PHRASE MATCH GAME FOR UNITS 1-3

is high.

15

cleans the air.

18

are efficient.

13

into the bin.

16

is an appliance.

17

a natural resource.

14

leave the lights on.

24

wastes water.

20

not true.

21

our environment.

23

is 2,000 pounds.

22

using again.

19

PHRASE MATCH GAME FOR UNITS 4-6

Containers hold 1	We should slash 7
Trash and garbage 2	Please read 8
Methane is 3	It's important 9
Styrofoam 4	Toxic products 10
Big trucks 5	There are four quarts 11
Landfills 6	Efficient cars 12

PHRASE MATCH GAME FOR UNITS 4-6

all kinds of things. 22	our trash. 24
fill landfills. 20	the warning labels. 17
a greenhouse gas. 18	to replace the filter. 19
lasts for years. 15	are dangerous. 16
haul waste. 13	in a gallon. 21
release methane. 23	burn less gas. 14

PHRASE MATCH GAME FOR UNITS 7-10

Tap water 1	Rainwater runs off 7
Spring water 2	It's necessary to 8
Please don't 3	Locavores eat 9
You can return 4	We should support 10
Tools are necessary 5	Our children 11
Plants grow better 6	Pesticides are used 12

Earth Matters ❀ Going Green

PHRASE MATCH GAME FOR UNITS 4-6

comes from a faucet. 15	into rivers and sewers. 24
comes from the ground. 22	weed your garden. 23
litter! 18	local food. 21
some empty bottles. 20	our local farmers. 16
for gardening. 13	deserve a healthy life. 19
with organic fertilizer. 17	to kill pests. 14

Earth Matters ❀ Going Green

WORD Match Game for Units 1-3

breathe 7	recreation 19
conserve 3	recycle 6
efficient 21	survive 13
energy 11	electric 17
pollutant 14	appliance 8
reuse 16	environment 24

WORD Match Game for Units 1-3

breath 12	recreational 10
conservation 2	recyclable 5
efficiency 9	survival 22
energetic 23	electricity 18
pollution 1	application 4
reusable 15	environmental 20

WORD Match Game for Units 4-6

fill 7	hazardous 10
container 3	inflation 22
contributor 17	option 4
dangerous 13	package 20
dependent 15	reduce 9
fatal 1	replace 23

WORD Match Game for Units 4-6

refill 19	hazard 8
contain 6	inflate 5
contribute 14	optional 16
danger 11	packaging 18
depend on 21	reduction 12
fatality 24	replacement 2

Earth Matters ❀ Going Green

WORD Match Game for Units 7-10

connect	informative
13	5
destruction	inspire
8	15
fertilizer	local
12	1
greedy	nutritious
9	10
healthy	pesticide
20	22
improve	produce
18	4

Earth Matters ❀ Going Green

WORD MATCH GAME FOR UNITS 7-10

connection 23	inform 16
destroy 2	inspiring 19
fertilize 24	locality 7
greed 17	nutrition 11
health 3	pest 14
improvement 21	production 6

				bin
			bulb	
		filter		
	ecosystem			
effort				

appliance	efficient	myth
big deal	electric	pollutant
to breathe	energy	to recycle
compact	to expel	to reuse
to conserve	fluorescent	throw away
critical	to last	wear and tear
eco-friendly	to leave on	wrapping paper

				faucet
			landfill	
		Styrofoam		
	package			
garbage				

biodegradable	dripping	to release
bottom line	to haul	resource
to conserve	impact	to slash
container	leak	to survive
contributor	precious	to take care of
to damage	recreation	trash
to decompose	to reduce	wastewater

BINGO GAME #3 FOR UNITS 5-6

				cleaning products
			gas guzzler	
		toxic		
	rush hour			
gallon				

to absorb	to dump	to inflate
to adopt	fatal	to inhale
allergy	to figure out	to replace
to burn	to fill	scent
to carpool	fresh	to sneeze
dangerous	hazardous	tremendous
dependent	idling	warning label

BINGO GAME #4 FOR UNITS 7-8

				fertilizer
			green thumb	
		litter		
	organic			
spring water				

bucket	to improve	to run off
to connect	to overflow	seeds
to decay	petroleum	sewer
to dig	to plant	to ship
empty	to produce	tap water
to give up	to provide	tool
healthy	to remain	to weed

Earth Matters ❀ Going Green

				locavore
			nutritious	
		organize		
	pesticide			
steward				

to alert	greedy	opportunity
to beat	to grow	to pick
boost	hero	research
complacent	informative	ripe
to deserve	inspiring	to spread
destruction	jail	to support
to find out	local	to taunt

Line-up #1
World's Largest Dams – to be done after Unit 1

Three Gorges, China	Tarbela, Pakistan
Syncrude Tailings, Canada	Kambaratinsk, Kyrgyzstan
Chapeton, Argentina	Fort Peck, US
Pati, Argentina	Lower Usuma, Nigeria
New Cornelia Tailings, US	Cipasang, Indonesia
Nagarjuna Sagar, India	Ataturk, Turkey

Direction: Line up according to the world's largest dams

Notes: Largest is in terms of most material (concrete, tailings, etc.).

Answers on page 76.

paper	nylon fabric
orange peels	tin cans
wool socks	aluminum cans
cigarette butts	plastic six-pack holder rings
plasticized milk cartons	glass bottles
leather shoes	plastic bottles

Direction: Line up according to the amount of time these things take to degrade.

Answers on page 76.

Earth Matters ❀ Going Green

LINE-UP #3
GAS MILEAGE (MPG) RATINGS – TO BE DONE AFTER UNIT 6

Toyota Yaris	Lexus
Chevrolet Cobalt	Chrysler Cruiser
Ford Focus	Ford Expedition
Honda Civic	Cadillac Escalade
Chevrolet Aveo	Jeep Grand Cherokee
Volkswagen Beetle	Dodge Ram 1500

Direction: Line up according to best miles per gallon.

Answers on page 77.

Line-up #4
Vegetables – the great and good

Kale	Green bell pepper
Spinach	Okra
Sweet potato	Avocado
Broccoli – raw	Potato with skin
Carrots – raw	Beets
Peas	Onion

Direction: Line up according to the best overall. (See notes in Answers)

Answers on page 77.

CROSSWORD #1 – TO BE DONE AFTER UNIT 3

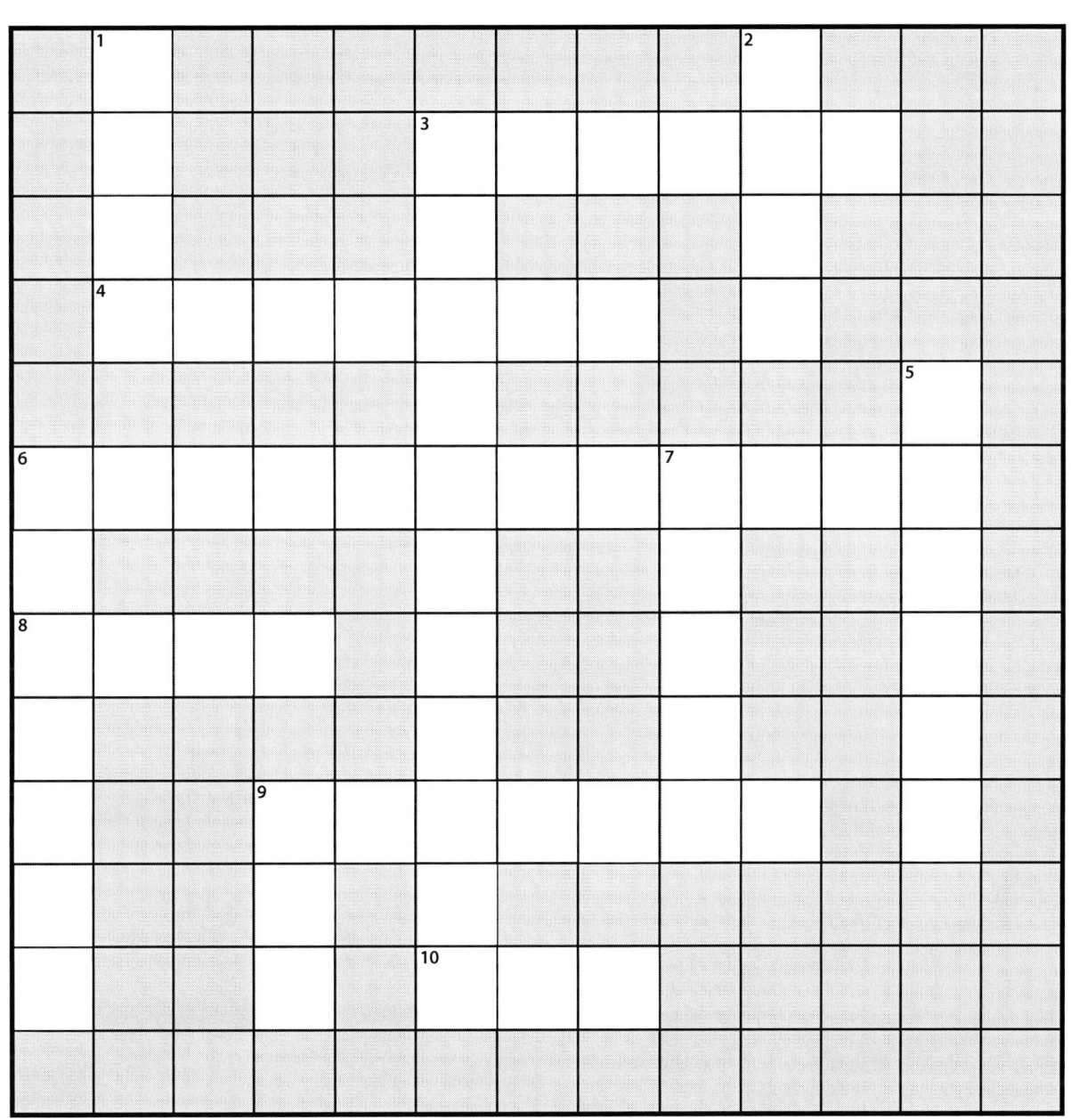

Across

3 To clean air, water, etc.
4 To make dirty
6 Saving something
8 It's not true
9 To take in and expel
10 2000 pounds

Down

1 A leaky faucet will do this.
2 It drips because there is a _____.
3 A kind of light bulb
5 We need it.
6 Small in size, like a car
7 We throw it out.
9 A container

Answers on page 78

Earth Matters ❀ Going Green

Across

  2 Four quarts
  4 Do something with something
  5 Automobile
  6 One is fluorescent
 10 A fire does it
 11 Cars burn it
 12 An SUV
 15 To throw away
 16 New or a kind of water
 18 To carry a load

Down

  1 Many pounds
  2 Food waste
  3 Make smaller
  7 A country
  8 A Volkswagen
  9 Dangerous
 13 Cut
 14 We do it with energy or money
 17 It gives heat and light

CROSSWORD #3 – TO BE DONE AFTER UNIT 10

Answers on page 78

Across

3 To get bigger
4 To make full
6 Wangari Maathai was put there
7 Something to help with work
9 It helps plants grow
12 A bucket with a hole in it will _____.
13 A kind of water
15 To decompose
16 Not from far away

Down

1 To get things together and ready
2 A chance to do something
4 Deadly
5 Roadside trash
8 To put seeds in the ground
10 You should eat fruit when it is _____.
11 A movement
14 Let's _____ some berries.

Verb Cards

last 1	reuse 2
leave on 1	conserve 3
breathe 2	damage 3
expel 2	survive 3
filter 2	take care of 3
recycle 2	haul 4

Verb Cards

decompose 4	dump 5
reduce 4	inhale 5
release 4	replace 5
slash 4	fill 6
package 4	figure out 6
absorb 5	burn 6

Verb Cards

carpool	ship
6	7
decay	connect
7	8
overflow	improve
7	8
remain	plant
7	8
litter	provide
7	8
produce	weed
7	8

Earth Matters: Going Green

Verb Cards

run off 8	taunt 10
find out 9	deserve 10
grow 9	jail 10
pick 9	organize 10
support 9	speak out 10
beat 10	spread the word 10

Earth Matters ❀ Going Green

1   What is a CFL?

a compact florescent light bulb

7   What does "walk your talk" mean?

do something, not only talk about it

2   What does compact mean?

small in size

8   What is "wear and tear"?

damage to something from repeated use

3   What are big bucks?

lots of money

9   Where does paper come from?

trees

4   What does "common myth" mean?

*It's something people believe,
but it isn't true.*

10 What is an eco-system?

everything in nature working as one unit

5   Which of these is not an appliance -- a computer, a TV, a car?

a car

11 What is deforestation?

cutting down large areas of forests

6   Name one way to be energy efficient.

turn off appliances when not in use

12 What is CO_2?

carbon dioxide

QUIZ CARDS – TO BE USED AFTER UNIT 5

13 Give one reason why trees are important.

They take in carbon dioxide, and expel oxygen.

19 What is trash?

things we throw away

14 What are pollutants in the air?

gases that make the air dirty

20 Why should trash be picked up at the beach?

because it could kill sea life

15 What is global warming?

an increase in world temperatures

21 Why is water a precious resource?

We cannot live without it.

16 What causes global warming?

an increase in carbon dioxide in the air

22 Why is a leaking faucet bad?

It wastes a lot of water.

17 What is H_2O?

water

23 What does conserve mean?

to keep or protect

18 What is garbage?

waste food stuff

24 What is the environment ?

everything around us

Earth Matters ❀ Going Green

Earth Matters ❀ Going Green

25 What does slash mean?

to cut or reduce

31 What is indoor pollution?

bad air inside a house or building

26 What is a landfill?

a place where waste is buried

32 What is a warning label?

information on a product about its dangers

27 What does decompose mean?

to decay

33 What does inhale mean?

to breathe in

28 What is Styrofoam?

a kind of packaging that doesn't decompose

34 What's another word for hazardous?

dangerous

29 What is methane?

a gas that contributes to global warming

35 What does fatal mean?

It causes death.

30 What is a greenhouse gas?

a gas that contributes to global warming

36 What does toxic mean?

poisonous and dangerous

Quiz Cards – to be used after Unit 10

1 What is a gas guzzler?

any vehicle that uses a lot of gas

7 What does mpg mean?

miles per gallon

2 What is idling?

running a car's engine but not moving

8 What is mph?

miles per hour

3 What is carpooling?

sharing a ride with other people

9 When is rush hour?

when people are coming or going to work

4 Why should tires be properly inflated?

to get good gas mileage

10 What is tap water?

water from the faucet

5 How many quarts are in a gallon?

four

11 Why are plastic water bottles bad for the environment?

They take hundreds of years to decay.

6 How do cars pollute the atmosphere?

they release carbon dioxide

12 Is bottled water always safer than tap water in the US?

No, it isn't.

Earth Matters ❀ Going Green

13 What is spring water?

water that comes out of the ground

14 Is all bottled water spring water?

No, some is filtered tap water.

15 What is litter?

anything thrown away in a public area

16 What does "environmentally-conscious" mean?

acting in ways that don't harm our planet

17 Are plastic bottles biodegradable?

No.

18 What do you use a bucket for?

carrying water

19 What is erosion?

washing away the soil

20 What is a green thumb?

the ability to grow things

21 What are seeds?

the part of a plant that can produce a new plant

22 What is weeding?

pulling up unwanted plants

23 What's the best kind of fertilizer?

organic fertilizer

24 What is a shrub?

a plant like a small bush

25 What does buying locally mean?

buying food grown in your area

31 Who was Rachael Carson?

*an environmentalist who
warned about pesticides*

26 Why is shopping locally better
for the environment?

*Locally-grown food doesn't travel
thousands of miles.*

32 What is a pest?

*an animal that causes problems
such as destroying plants*

27 What is a locavore?

someone who eats local food

33 What famous book did Rachel Carson
write?

Silent Spring

28 Why is buying locally good economically?

the money stays in the community

34 Who is Wangari Maathai?

the "mother" of the Green Movement in Kenya

29 Are local markets more expensive?

Sometimes.

35 What prize did Wangari Maathai win?

the Nobel Peace Prize

30 What is a ripe fruit?

a fruit ready to be eaten; not green

36 Who was Chico Mendes?

*a Brazilian who tried to stop the
deforestation of the Amazon Rainforest*

Earth Matters & Going Green

Answers for the Line-ups

Answers for Line-up #1 on page 59

Three Gorges, China
Syncrude Tailings, Canada
Chapeton, Argentina
Pati, Argentina
New Cornelia Tailings, US
Nagarjuna Sagar, India
Tarbela, Pakistan
Kambaratinsk, Kyrgyzstan
Fort Peck, US
Lower Usuma, Nigeria
Cipasang, Indonesia
Ataturk, Turkey

Note: Largest is in terms of most material (concrete, tailings, etc.).

Answers for Line-up #2 on page 60

paper, *2 – 5 months*
orange peels, *6 months*
wool socks, *1 – 5 years*
cigarette butts, *1 – 12 years*
plasticized milk cartons, *5 years*
leather shoes, *25 – 40 years*
nylon fabric, *30 – 40 years*
tin cans, *50 – 100 years*
aluminum cans, *80 – 100 years*
plastic six-pack holder rings, *450 years*
glass bottles, *1 million years*
plastic bottles, *forever*

ANSWERS FOR THE LINE-UPS

Answers for Line-up #3 on page 61

Toyota Yaris 36
Chevrolet Cobalt 35
Ford Focus 35
Honda Civic 34
Chevrolet Aveo 34
Volkswagen Beetle 29
Lexus 26
Chrysler Cruiser 24
Ford Expedition 20
Cadillac Escalade 14
Jeep Grand Cherokee 14
Dodge Ram Pick-up 1500 13

Note: 2009 models
Source: **www.greenautochoice.com**

Answers for Line-up #4 on page 62

	SCORE
Kale	1,389
Spinach	931
Sweet potato	485
Broccoli – raw	420
Carrots – raw	348
Peas	166
Green bell pepper	111
Okra	85
Avocado	73
Potato with skin	53
Beets	38
Onion	19

Source: Nutrition Action Newsletter, January-February, 2009

Note: Scores are a total based on scores for nutrients, fiber, lutein/carotenoids, vitamins C and K, folic acid, potassium, calcium, iron

ANSWERS FOR THE CROSSWORDS

CROSSWORD #1 – TO BE DONE AFTER UNIT 3
Puzzle on pages 63

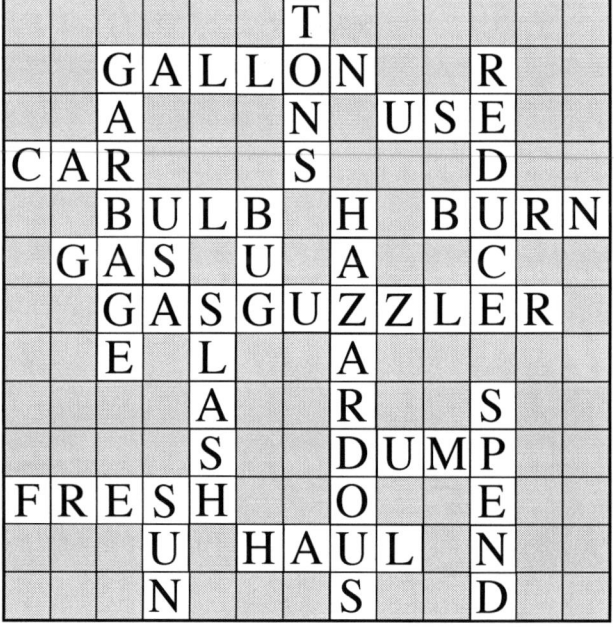

CROSSWORD #2 – TO BE DONE AFTER UNIT 6
Puzzle on pages 64

CROSSWORD #3 – TO BE DONE AFTER UNIT 10
Puzzle on pages 65